Responsible Pet Care

Dogs

Responsible Pet Care

Dogs

PAM JAMESON

Rourke Publications, Inc.
Vero Beach, FL 32964

Library of Congress Cataloging-in-Publication Data

Jameson, Pam, 1942-
  Dogs/by Pam Jameson.

    p. cm - (Responsible pet care)
  Includes index.
  Summary: Examines the different varieties of dogs and describes
how they may be housed, fed, handled, exercised, cleaned, and bred.
  ISBN 0-86625-184-7
  1. Dogs - Juvenile literature. [1. Dogs.] I. Title.
II. Series: Responsible pet care (Vero Beach, Fla.)
SF426.5.J26 1989
636.7'0887-dc19   88-31295
                 CIP
                 AC

CONTENTS

1 Why Choose A Dog?   6

2 Varieties   8

3 Buying A Puppy   10

4 Visiting The Veterinarian   13

5 Shopping For Essentials   15

6 Early Days And House Training   17

7 Training   19

8 Feeding   22

9 Cleaning And Grooming   24

10 Travel   26

11 Breeding   28

12 Health And Longevity   29

    Glossary   30

    Index   31

Why Choose A Dog?

If you have always wanted a dog of your own, the "someday" that you have been promised can seem very far away. Perhaps you have been told that you must wait until you are older or until your family moves to a larger house or one with a yard. Let's suppose that the great day has come at last, and you can now look for that dog you have always wanted.

All your friends, whether they are dog owners or not, will be anxious to tell you how to find a dog. Before you go any further, though, it is best to ask yourself two important questions: Why do you want a dog? Will you be a good and responsible dog owner?

A dog will very rapidly become part of your family.

This German shepherd puppy, often known as an Alsatian, will grow very quickly. Can your home cope with a very large dog?

The best and most sensible reason for getting a dog is that you will enjoy it. You are gaining a friend and companion, and, if you are willing to take the opportunity, you will learn a great deal about the world of dogs.

In becoming a dog owner, you are volunteering to look after another living creature for its whole life. Your dog will depend on you for food, shelter, medical attention, and affection. If you start with a young puppy, you will have to teach it how to behave so it can become an accepted member of your family. You must be sure that you and your family have the time, space, and money to supply all these needs.

Varieties

You may already have a firm idea of the kind of dog you want. Perhaps you want a dog like your neighbors have or like one you have seen in a movie. Lots of collies owe their popularity to Lassie. You may already know whether you want a **mongrel** or a **purebred** dog. It is still best to take a look at all the possibilities before making a choice. Look at as many different **breeds** as possible and find out how they differ, not only in size and appearance but also in character. Even if you choose a mongrel, or a mixed breed, you'll need to know about the different characteristics it displays. For several years now, the cocker spaniel has been America's most popular dog. In the largest breeds, you will find that the German shepherd, doberman, Labrador retriever, boxer, rottweiler, dalmation, and collie are also popular. Favorite medium-sized breeds include beagles, dachshunds, and many different varieties of spitz, spaniels, setters, pointers, and terriers. Among the very small breeds, some classed as toys, you will find toy poodles, Yorkshire terriers, pugs, Pekinese, bichon frise, Chihuahuas, miniature dachshunds, and schnauzers.

If you decide you want a purebred dog, try to go to a dog show, where you will be able to see many different breeds at once. Imagine how each dog would fit into your home. Talk to the owners (but not just as they are going into the ring to be judged). Most breeders are concerned that their puppies go to suitable homes, and they would probably ask you several questions as a prospective owner.

When you have narrowed down your choices, look in the local papers for kennels or breeders who are advertising puppies. Many advertisements include the price, but you may have to call for the price on others. Make appointments to see the puppies you are interested in.

A **pedigree** is no guarantee that a puppy will grow into a champion. A pedigree tells you only the names of the dam (mother) and sire (father) of the pups for several generations, with perhaps a list of their show awards. For the pedigree to have any value, it must have been registered at the **American Kennel Club**. For every potential show winner, there will be half a dozen pet puppies, priced below the show quality animals.

Your next step is to decide whether you want a male or a female pup. Each sex has advantages and disadvantages. Many people believe that female dogs are more easily trained and more home loving. Males tend to roam in search of adventure.

For many years the cocker spaniel has been America's most popular dog.

Buying A Puppy

Since having a dog is a family decision, other members of your family will probably want to accompany you on your search. If you can take someone with you who is knowledgeable about dogs, so much the better. Look carefully at the puppies you are offered and also at their surroundings. Dog kennels should not have a bad smell. Ask to see the mother of the litter – this will give you a good idea of what the youngsters will look like when they grow up.

A healthy puppy should be full of curiosity and will want to come toward you. Its eyes will be clear, and it will be neither too fat nor too thin. No ribs or backbone should show. At this age, the coat can be ragged and uneven in some breeds, but there should be no bare patches. Be very suspicious of constant scratching or head shaking. Never choose a miserable, sickly looking puppy just because you feel sorry for it. If you have any

At one month old, this golden retriever is still not ready to leave its mother.

10

Healthy puppies are eager for their food. They should be neither too fat nor too thin and should have clean, shiny coats.

doubts about your choice, ask the breeder if a veterinarian can see the puppy before you agree to buy it. Most breeders will be satisfied with this arrangement and will supply you with details of any **inoculations** which your puppy has had. You should also get a diet sheet and a note of any worming treatments that have been given.

Don't be too disappointed if you cannot take your puppy away with you right away. Puppies are often advertised when they are about six weeks old, and many breeders prefer to keep the litter for eight weeks. They keep very small breeds until they are ten weeks old.

If you do not want a purebred dog, a healthy mongrel, or mixed breed dog, can make a very good companion. Mongrels often have a combination of the characteristics of several breeds.

Humane societies and dog pounds always have animals that need new homes. If you're lucky you can get a healthy animal and at the same time save it from being destroyed as unwanted. Many of these dogs, however, will be incurable wanderers who have run away from home once too often. Others, perhaps, have been untrainable and have strained the patience of their previous owners. Still others are there because their owners had to move and could not take their dog with them. Sometimes remarks are noted on a card by the cage: "Is not house trained" or "Chews furniture." Many puppies, however, end up at a pound or humane society simply because the owner could not find homes for all of them.

Don't forget that a small puppy can grow very large. Make sure you have a good idea of the puppy's size when full-grown – for mongrels, this will depend on the mother and father's size. If you have a small apartment with little or no yard, do not choose a large dog.

If you have a cat, be prepared for a little difficulty at first. Some cats will want to play mother to a young puppy, but others will be quite jealous. If you have small caged pets, such as gerbils, be sure that they are placed safely out of reach. The same is true for bird cages and aquariums.

Look carefully at the way the puppies are looked after by the breeder. Good dog kennels do not have a bad smell.

Visiting The Veterinarian

Your puppy's first visit to the vet should come soon after you bring your puppy home, especially if it has not already had its first set of shots. Puppies have an inherited protection from their mother against some canine diseases, but the level of resistance falls as they are weaned. Modern medicine can protect your dog against most of the diseases with which it is likely to come in contact. Among those are distemper, hepatitis, leptospirosis, parvo virus, and rabies. It is important to begin inoculations against these diseases as soon as possible and to keep your puppy from other dogs until it is fully protected. You will be given a record card showing the dates when **boosters** are required.

The vet will also test your puppy's lungs and look at its eyes and ears with special instruments. The vet may take its temperature and ask you to hold the puppy firmly for its inoculation. Your puppy may be feeling scared, so it is important that you stay calm and confident and speak cheerfully during the shot or examination.

Puppies have some natural immunity from their mother. This border collie is now old enough to have shots that will protect him against several canine diseases.

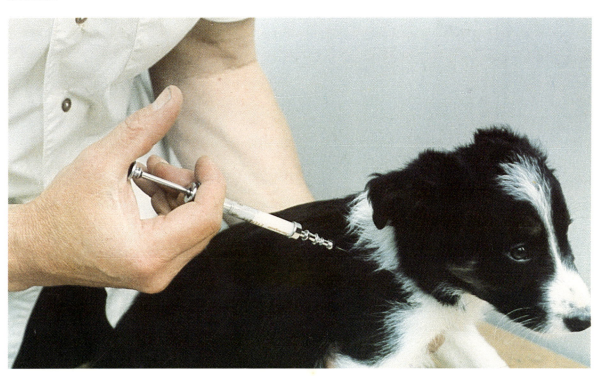

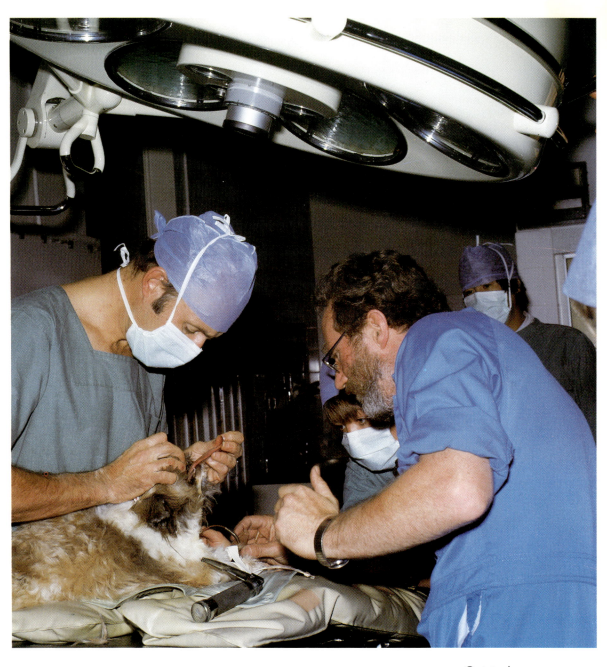

Many puppies have intestinal **worms** – tiny worms that live as **parasites** inside the dog. Your veterinarian will check your puppy, and if it has worms, will treat them with medicine. More and more dogs in North America are also getting heartworm. This worm, which lives in a dog's heart, will kill the dog if it is not treated. Today, there are pills to prevent heartworm, but they must be given regularly during the heartworm season.

Get to know your veterinarian. On your first visit he or she will answer any questions you may have about how to take care of your dog.

Shopping For Essentials

As soon as you bring your puppy or dog home, you must have certain supplies ready. First is food. What should you feed your new pet?

Food and Dishes

If you bought your dog from a breeder, he or she will supply you with instructions on what kind of food it needs. Commercial dog food made especially for puppies is nutritionally balanced and adequate for most puppies. Your veterinarian may advise extra vitamins, especially for fast growing puppies. When buying a feeding dish, choose one suited to the size of your puppy. Earthenware, stainless steel, and heavy duty plastic are all good choices. Buy a separate bowl for water and be sure that it is heavy enough not to tip over.

Bed

Your puppy or dog will need somewhere to sleep, other than in your bed. A cardboard box with a blanket inside can serve the purpose for a new puppy. As it grows older, you might want to buy a dog bed. A molded plastic bed is unchewable, and you can add a washable cushion or a blanket to make it softer. Basket-style beds are also popular for small and medium-sized dogs.

An earthenware feeding dish is easy to clean and will not be easily tipped over.

Collar and Leash

Get your puppy used to wearing a collar right away. The collar should be soft and not fit too tightly. You should be able to slip two fingers beneath it comfortably. Attach an ID tag with your name and address to the collar (available by mail order from many dog food companies). Check a puppy's collar size occasionally, since it will soon outgrow it.

You will probably want a leash right away too. Later, when you begin training your dog in obedience, you will want a sturdy leather leash. The size of the leash will depend on your dog's size. For now, you can use any small leash.

Other Items

If you have a long-haired dog, you will need a brush or comb suited to its particular type of coat. Ask the person at the pet store which kind is best for your dog. Something to chew is also essential. In the beginning, choose a hide bone or a toy to keep teeth and gums in good condition. These are often meaty and are safer than bones from the butcher.

Get your puppy used to wearing a light collar and leash. Later on you will need a training collar.

Early Days and House Training

A young puppy will want to explore its new surroundings. To begin with, it will miss the comfort of its mother and the other puppies in the litter. For the first two or three days, it will need lots of reassurance from you. It is a good idea to get a puppy when you have extra time to give to it – perhaps during a long weekend or a school vacation. Puppies need a lot of sleep, so put its bed in a corner of the house, out of the traffic flow. A few sheets of newspaper around its bed will protect the floor from any accidents. If you can't be on hand all the time, a puppy kennel is useful. Puppies feel secure in these kennels, and usually curl up and go to sleep.

When your puppy finds itself all alone for the first night in a new home, it may decide to let everyone in the neighborhood know that it is not happy. Although a howling puppy can keep everyone awake, do not be tempted to take it into bed beside you. If the night is cold, put a well-wrapped hot water bottle into its bed or kennel along with an old cuddly toy or even a bundle of soft clothes – something that it can snuggle up to.

House training

House training takes time and patience. A puppy's instinct is to be clean, so you must watch for the signals that it wants to relieve itself. These usually consist of whining or turning round and sniffing at the ground. This is the moment to carry it quickly outside or onto the newspaper provided. You must then stay with it until it has finished. Don't dump your puppy outside the door and leave it. It will probably sit on the step until you open the door and then dash into the house and do its business – just what you didn't want to happen! Praise your puppy when it goes outside or on the newspaper, but never punish or scold when it has an accident. Rubbing your puppy's nose in its own mess is cruel and unnecessary and will frighten your puppy. You can buy training aids in liquid form. A few drops on a piece of newspaper will encourage the puppy to go to that spot.

Early Days And House Training

Give your puppy a name, and use that name as often as possible. When it is time for training, only one person should work with the dog. This person will probably be you.

When your dog knows his or her name, you must next teach the word "no." This means "Stop what you are doing – it is not allowed." One sharp command is sufficient. In the beginning, you will have to show your puppy what "no" means as you say it. If it is trying to jump up on you, for example, push the dog down firmly as you say "No."

Let your puppy wear a collar for a short time each day. After the first few days, attach the leash. Some puppies try to play tug-of-war with the leash, but do not turn this into a play session. Discourage bad habits right from the start, and lay down firm rules of acceptable and unacceptable behavior. It may be amusing to see a young puppy pulling at curtains or chewing slippers, but unless your dog understands that this is forbidden, he or she will grow up to do the same thing. Not everybody likes dogs. You may not mind if your pet jumps up and tries to lick your face, but when a dog puts muddy paws all over a visitor or a stranger, neither of you will be very popular.

This cocker spaniel has its own toys and is less likely to chew on slippers and furniture.

Training

Set aside a short period every day as your puppy's school time. Ten minutes is enough. For training, you should buy a training collar – a chain with rings at either end that forms a collar when the chain is slipped through one of the rings. Aim at teaching just three basic commands: "Sit," "Stay," and "Come." Do not be discouraged if it takes many weeks to get perfect results.

Training is very important, and it can even be enjoyable. Short sessions of ten minutes are enough to begin with.

For the command "Sit," hold the leash in your right hand and gently press down on the dog's hind quarters with your left hand. At the same time, say "Sit." When he or she is in the correct position, stroke and praise your dog. When your dog will sit on command without having to be pushed, he or she is ready to learn "Stay." Make your dog sit and then say "Stay." Move a couple of feet in front of the dog, still holding onto the leash. If the dog tries to follow, you say "No" firmly and repeat the word "Stay." Repeat this process moving farther away from the dog each time. From this position you can progress to "Come" in a quick cheerful tone by pulling your dog gently toward you on the leash.

Most towns and cities have dog training classes where these and other commands are taught. Whether or not you intend to enter your dog in dog shows, obedience training is very important. Not only does it make your dog easier to handle, it also helps create a special bond between you and your dog.

Your dog will love to accompany you on a walk through the woods. You can trust a well trained dog to come back when off the leash.

20

All dogs need activity and interest in their lives, just as we do. Daily walks can provide the activity for some dogs. Others may need to run in an open space. Even very small breeds can find lots of interest if they are allowed to explore different rooms in an apartment or have the free run of a safe balcony. Exciting games of hide and seek or throwing a ball can provide all the exercise needed.

In most cities and towns, it is against the law to leave your dog's droppings anywhere – in the street, on the sidewalk, or in a park. A responsible owner will clean up after his own dog with a "pooper scooper" and a plastic bag.

This Old English sheepdog has fun playing with its owner.

Feeding

You can combine some of your dog's early training with feeding time. As you rattle your dog's dish, call him or her by name. The dog will soon connect its own name and the word "come" with a pleasant experience.

You can choose from a wide range of commercial dog foods, but read the list of ingredients to find out if the food you select is nutritionally complete.

Always keep the food and water bowl in the same place. The water bowl should be washed out and refilled each day. For at least the first week, stick to the breeder's diet sheet, if you have one. Otherwise, feed your puppy a commercial food made especially for puppies. Dogs require a mixed diet, one that contains proteins as well as carbohydrates, fats, minerals, and vitamins. As your pup grows, you may find that, just as you prefer certain foods, so does your pup. While many working or hunting dogs will be content to eat the same food every day, dogs that are part of a household should be offered a wide variety of foods.

Some owners still prefer to buy meat or offal such as heart, kidney, and liver and feed this either raw or cooked. The majority of dog owners use the more convenient dog foods sold in grocery stores. Animal nutritionists have worked closely with dog food manufacturers to produce a great number of different dog diets. Read the list of contents to find out whether you need to add anything. Look for food that is listed as "nutritionally complete and balanced" to make sure your dog gets all the essential elements it needs.

The amount of food varies according to the dog, as does the number of feeds a day. In general, puppies up to three months are fed three or four times a day. At six months, twice a day is usually sufficient, and by one year most dogs will eat one main meal. Your dog should always be ready for his meal but not worrying and begging for food long before it is due. Many dogs who are overfed by anxious owners become overweight, a fact that will certainly shorten their lives. Do not feed your dog from the table, and keep tid-bits and dog treats as a reward for good behavior or as a training aid. Any uneaten food should be taken away if it is not eaten in fifteen minutes. Dogs have a highly developed sense of smell and will often refuse to eat food that has gone stale.

While many dogs will miss an occasional meal without any ill effects, you should consult your veterinarian if this continues for more than a couple of days. If your dog is eating everything you offer and still remains very thin, here again you should seek expert advice.

Cleaning And Grooming

Very few dogs actually enjoy being groomed or bathed, but they will submit as long as the process is not too long or too painful.

A little attention every day is better than a lot once a week, so keep the brush and comb where you can find it easily and use it regularly. Some long-haired breeds, such as poodles, need to have their coats thinned down or clipped off at intervals to keep them manageable. This is a job best left to the expert. Always ask what the cost is likely to be before you book an appointment with the dog groomer. If the coat is badly matted or has been neglected, removing it can be very expensive.

Even the best cared for dog can pick up fleas or ticks. Check your dog's coat periodically for fleas. Fleas leave a residue on the skin, so check for small black specks. If your dog goes into the woods during the tick season, check very carefully every night for ticks. If you find a tick you can remove it with a pair of tweezers, making sure that you remove the head as well. Pet shops sell anti-flea and anti-tick powders, sprays, and anti-flea collars to protect your dog. Don't forget to treat your dog's bedding as well.

A special anti-flea shampoo can give you a head start. Bathe your dog at home either in the tub or under the shower. A small dog can be bathed in the sink or in bowls of water. Ask a friend or family member to help you. You will probably get wet during the process, and two pairs of hands are better than one. If you work quickly and calmly, your dog will not be too nervous. Take care that none of the soapy water goes into the dog's eyes or ears. Rinse very well, and dry thoroughly with a rough towel or with a hair dryer. Never let the dog out into the yard to dry off, since he or she will just head for the nearest patch of mud and roll in it. A dog's claws should just touch or be clear of the ground. Many dogs wear down their claws by walking on concrete sidewalks, but others need clipping. Dew claws, which grow on the side or the back of the leg, also need clipping occasionally. Your pet shop or veterinarian can cut back the claws for you.

When you bath your dog, work quickly and calmly.

24

Travel

Most dogs love going places, even if it is only for a walk around the block. Dogs usually also love to travel by car. If your parents will permit it, take your puppy on very short car rides to begin with, and ride in the back seat with the dog.

Small dogs travel best in a kennel with an open wire front. A larger dog should wear a harness firmly anchored to the car seat. Food is only necessary if you are going on a long trip, but take a container of water, a drinking bowl, and a supply of newspapers in case of accidents. In hot weather, make sure that the car is well ventilated, but do not let your dog put its head out an open window. Never leave a dog alone in a car with all the windows closed in direct sunlight or where the sun may come around later in the day. A dog in this situation can easily suffocate. If your dog is a poor traveler and you plan to take it on a family trip, your veterinarian will suggest a tranquilizer to be given a few hours before the start of your journey.

Small dogs feel more secure in a travel kennel with an open wire front.

In hot weather, never leave your dog in a car without ventilation.

If you cannot take your dog with you, perhaps a friend or neighbor will be able to take care of your pet. Your dog might stay with your friend's family or a neighbor can visit your dog to play with it, feed it, and walk it. Otherwise, your pet shop, veterinarian, or telephone directory will list some kennels that board dogs. When calling to check prices, also ask if the dogs are walked and allowed to run and play during certain periods, and any other questions you may think of that concern your dog.

Breeding

If you have a female puppy, she will begin coming into heat twice a year when she reaches seven or eight months. At that time, she may stop eating and try very hard to get outside to be mated. You must keep her away from male dogs during this time. It is irresponsible to let her breed unless you are positive that you can find good homes for all her puppies. Some large dogs can have ten or twelve puppies in one litter. Your family can be spared a good deal of trouble and expense if you make sure to neuter your female dog. This operation is called **spaying** and should be performed when your dog is between six and nine months old. Male dogs, too, can be **neutered** at this time if you are not intending to breed them.

This Rhodesian ridgeback is proud of her litter, but will they all go to good homes?

Health And Longevity

Your dog cannot tell you in words when he or she is in pain, but you will be able to tell from its behavior. It may whine or cry at your touch or refuse to come out of a corner even for food. It may lose its appetite, cough a lot, or throw up. All or any of these things are signs that your pet is sick and should be seen as soon as possible by a veterinarian.

Most dogs live for ten or twelve years, and many go on even longer. Failing hearing and eyesight are often the first signs of old age. An elderly dog will want fewer walks and smaller amounts of food more freqently. There is no need to end an animal's life just because it has grown old, but no dog owner wants to see a pet suffer. If you know that your dog is suffering and will not get better, the very last thing you can do for your friend is to let the veterinarian put it to sleep. This is never an easy decision, but it is a part of being a good dog owner and a very small price to pay for years of affection and companionship.

An elderly dog will need less exercise than a young dog.

GLOSSARY

American Kennel Club — An organization for dog owners and breeders.

Boosters — Additional injections that strengthen the effect of inoculations.

Breed — A group of dogs with the same physical characteristics.

Humane Society — A society concerned with the welfare and proper care of animals.

Inoculations — Injections given to animals to build up a resistance to various diseases.

Mongrel — A dog whose parents were of different breeds.

Neutered — A minor surgical procedure that alters or removes an animal's reproductive organs so he or she cannot have offspring.

Parasites — Organisms like worms or fleas that live on the blood of other animals.

Pedigree — A certificate with details of a dog's parents and grandparents that proves its breeding.

Purebred — A dog that comes from an unbroken line of one recognized breed.

Spaying — A simple operation that prevents a bitch from having puppies.

Worms — Parasites that are sometimes found in a dog's intestines.

INDEX

American Kennel Club	9
Bathing	24
Beds	15, 17
Bones	16
Breeding	28
Breeds	8, 10, 11, 21
Brushes	16, 24
Cats	12
Claws	24
Collars	16, 18, 19, 24
Combs	16, 24
Dew claws	24
Diet	11, 23
Diseases	13
Ears	13, 24
Exercise	21
Eyes	10, 13, 24
Feeding	22-23, 29
Female dogs	9, 28
Fleas	24
Food	15, 23, 26, 29
Grooming	24
Heat	28

Heartworm	14
House training	17, 18
Inoculations	11, 13
Kennels	8, 10, 17, 26, 27
Leashes	16, 18, 20
Male dogs	9, 28
Names	18
Neutering	28
Pedigree	9
Pet shops	24, 27
Spaying	28
Ticks	24
Training	18, 19-21, 22, 23
Travel	26
Veterinarian	11, 13-14, 15, 23, 24, 26, 27, 29
Walks	26, 27, 29
Water	23, 24, 26
Worms	14

We would like to thank and acknowledge the following people for the use of their photographs and transparencies:

Cover	Hans Reinhard/Bruce Coleman Ltd
Title Page	Hans Reinhard/Bruce Coleman Ltd
P. 6/7	Sally Anne Thompson/Animal Photography
P. 8/9	George McCarthy/Bruce Coleman Ltd
P. 10/11/12	Jane Burton/Bruce Coleman Ltd Marc Henrie ASC Sally Anne Thompson/Animal Photography Ltd
P. 13/14	Sally Anne Thompson/RSPCA Fritz Prenzel/Bruce Coleman Ltd
P. 15/18	Sally Anne Thompson/Animal Photography Ltd Marc Henrie ASC
P. 18	Sally Anne Thompson/Animal Photography
P. 19/20/21	Sally Anne Thompson/Animal Photography Ltd J P Ferrero/Ardea London Ltd Sally Anne Thompson/Animal Photography Ltd
P. 23	Ardea London Ltd
P. 25	Jane Burton/Bruce Coleman Ltd
P. 26/27	Sally Anne Thompson /Animal Photography Ltd Spectrum Colour Library/Anne Cumbers
P. 28	Sally Anne Thompson/Animal Photography Ltd
P. 29	Ardea London Ltd